NARCISSISTIC ABUSE RECORVERY FOR MEN

NARCISSISTIC ABUSE RECORVERY FOR MEN

A Men's Guide to Overcoming the Trauma bond, Dependency, Gaslighting, Manipulation and Reclaiming Your Self-essence.

GISLHAINE CHERY

<u>Disclaimer:</u>

- This book is not a substitute for professional help.

- The information in this book is for general purposes only. The author is not a licensed personal caregiver, healthcare provider, or medical professional. Always seek professional advice for specific concerns.

Dedication

To my dear sister Carmel for her constant support, boundless love, and profound understanding during my healing journey after surviving narcissistic abuse and navigating Serious emotional challenges.

With all my love and gratitude,

Gislhaine

TABLE OF CONTENTS

PAGES

INTRODUCTION 11

Why Focus on Men 13-14

What You Will Find in This Workbook?......... 15-16

1. UNDERSTANDING NARCISSISTIC ABUSE

- Key Insights on Narcissism 17-20
- Challenges Faced by Men 21

2. RECOGNIZING THE SIGNS

- Red Flags 23-26
- Emotional Impact 27-28
- Personal Stories 28-31
- Men's Unique Experiences 32

3. BREAKING FREE

- Identifying the Signs and preparing to leave.... 33-35
- Legal and Safety Considerations….................... 35
- Emotional Preparation 35-36

4. HEALING AND RECOVERY

- o Healing Components 37-39
- o Rebuilding Confidence 39
- o Reconnecting with Your self-essence 39-40
- o Building Support Network 40
- o Breaking Down Barriers to 41-43

5. REBUILDING YOUR LIFE

- o Establishing Boundaries 45-46
- o Reconnecting with Passions 46
- o Building Support System 47
- o Personal Growth 47-48
- o Creating a Fulfilling Future 48

6. MOVING FORWARD

- o Tips for Moving Forward 51-52
- o Building Healthy Relationships 52
- o Embracing Personal Growth 53-54
- o Exercises for Men 55-56

7. CONCLUSION 57-58

8. APPENDICES

- Self-Reflection Worksheets 59-61
- Journaling Prompts 62-63
- Affirmations and Positive Quotes...................... 64-65
- Frequents asked questions...........................66-67

INTRODUCTION

Welcome to **" Narcissistic Abuse Recovery"**. This book is a journey of understanding, healing, and growth. Whether you are currently in a relationship with a narcissist, have recently left one, or are still grappling with the aftermath, this guide is here to support you.

Narcissistic abuse can leave deep emotional and psychological scars. The manipulation, control, and devaluation inflicted by a narcissist can shatter your sense of self-worth and leave you feeling lost and alone. But there is hope. You have the power to heal, rebuild, and reclaim your life.

This book is a testament to the strength and resilience of survivors like you. It is filled with practical advice, powerful insights, and inspiring stories to help you navigate your recovery journey. Together, we will explore the dynamics of narcissistic abuse, recognize the signs, and develop strategies for healing and moving forward.

Remember, you are not alone in this journey. By picking up this book, you have taken a brave step towards understanding and recovery. Allow yourself the time and space to heal, and know that you have the strength within you to create a brighter, healthier future.

Thank you for trusting me to be a part of your healing journey.

Let's begin this transformative process together.

With compassion and hope,

Gislhaine

WHY FOCUS ON MEN

1. While narcissistic abuse affects individuals of all genders, men often face unique challenges in recognizing and addressing abuse due to societal expectations and stereotypes about masculinity. Men are often expected to be strong, self-reliant, and unemotional, which can make it difficult for them to acknowledge their vulnerability and seek help.

2. Men may also face stigma and disbelief when they share their experiences of abuse. This can lead to feelings of isolation and helplessness, as they may feel that their experiences are invalid or minimized. This book aims to address these unique challenges and provide a supportive resource for men recovering from narcissistic abuse.

By focusing on the specific experiences and needs of men, this book seeks to:

1. **Raise Awareness:** Educate men about the signs and effects of narcissistic abuse.

2. **Provide Support:** Offer practical strategies for breaking free from abusive relationships and beginning the healing process.

3. **Foster Community:** Create a sense of solidarity and support among men who have experienced narcissistic abuse.

4. **Promote Healing:** Provide guidance on the emotional and psychological recovery process.

WHAT YOU'LL FIND IN THIS BOOK

Understanding Narcissistic Abuse. This book provides a comprehensive understanding of narcissistic abuse, detailing its dynamics and the cycle of manipulation. You will gain insight into the behavior patterns of narcissists and how these patterns affect victims emotionally and mentally.

Recognizing the Signs. By learning to identify the red flags and warning signs of narcissistic behavior, you will become more attuned to the subtle and overt tactics used by narcissists. This awareness is the first step towards breaking free from the cycle of abuse.

Practical Strategies for Breaking Free. You will find actionable steps to safely end their relationships with narcissists. This includes practical advice on legal and safety considerations, ensuring that they can extricate themselves from these toxic relationships with confidence and security.

Healing Emotional Wounds. This book offers a variety of strategies for emotional healing, emphasizing the importance of self-care and self-compassion. You will discover techniques to rebuild your self-esteem and confidence, empowering you to move forward with strength and resilience.

Rebuilding Your Life. With a focus on establishing healthy boundaries and reconnecting with oneself, you will learn how to rebuild your life after narcissistic abuse. This book provides guidance on finding new passions, nurturing positive relationships, and creating a supportive network.

Preventing Future Abuse. To avoid falling into similar patterns, this book offers tips on recognizing potential narcissistic traits in future relationships. You will be equipped with the knowledge to make informed decisions and foster healthier connections.

Personal Growth and Fulfillment. Ultimately, this book is a tool for personal growth and self-discovery. You will be encouraged to embrace their journey towards healing, recognizing your own strength and resilience. By the end of this book, you will have a clearer vision of a happier, healthier, and more fulfilling future.

Worksheets and Practical Tools. This book includes practical tools such as worksheets, journaling prompts, and affirmations. These resources provide you with a hands-on approach to track their progress, reflect on your experiences, and reinforce positive changes.

1

Understanding Narcissistic Abuse

Narcissistic abuse is a pervasive and insidious form of emotional and psychological manipulation inflicted by individuals with narcissistic traits or Narcissistic Personality Disorder (NPD). Understanding the nature of this abuse is essential for recognizing its impact and finding the path to healing.

1. The Essence of Narcissistic Abuse

Narcissistic abuse is characterized by a range of manipulative behaviors intended to control, demean, and exploit the victim. This abuse is not always obvious; it often manifests in subtle, covert ways that can leave the victim doubting their own perceptions and reality. The abuser seeks to dominate the victim's life, eroding their sense of self-worth and autonomy.

2. Traits of a Narcissist

To understand narcissistic abuse, it's important to recognize the traits commonly associated with narcissists. These traits can help identify the abusive behavior:

- Need for excessive admiration
- Triangulation
- Exploitation of others
- Envy
- Unrealistic Expectations
- Self-perception of uniqueness
- Sense of superiority
- Interpersonal difficulties
- Difficulty accepting criticism
- Manipulative behavior
- Constant need for attention
- Fragile self-esteem
- Lack of genuine relationships
- Inflation of accomplishments
- Quick to anger
- Tendency to blame others
- Obsessive need for control
- Superficial charm
- Inconsistent behavior
- Difficulty managing emotions
- Pathological lying
- Overstepping limits

- Prone to jealousy
- Difficulty with teamwork
- Impatience
- Chronic dissatisfaction
- Self-centered decision-making
- Love-bombing
- Lack of remorse
- Love of drama
- Dependency on external validation
- Paranoia
- Tendency to exploit others
- Fear of being exposed
- Selective listening
- Tendency to belittle others
- Difficulty with authority
- Need for instant gratification
- Inability to apologize
- Unforgiving nature
- Self-victimization
- Difficulty accepting reality
- Irresponsibility
- Tendency to dominate conversations
- Indifference to others' suffering

The Cycle of Narcissistic Abuse

Narcissistic abuse often follows a predictable cycle, which can make it difficult for victims to break free. The cycle typically includes three stages:

a) **Idealization**: In this initial stage, the narcissist lavishes the victim with praise, affection, and attention. This period, known as "love bombing," creates a deep emotional attachment and dependence. The victim feels valued and cherished, which reinforces the bond with the narcissist.

b) **Devaluation**: Over time, the narcissist's behavior shifts. They begin to criticize, belittle, and undermine the victim. This stage is marked by emotional manipulation and abusive tactics. The victim's self-esteem and confidence are systematically eroded, making them more dependent on the narcissist.

c) **Discard**: Eventually, the narcissist may abruptly end the relationship or emotionally withdraw. This stage can be devastating for the victim, leaving them feeling abandoned, confused, and worthless. The discard often happens without warning, further destabilizing the victim.

CHALLENGES FACED BY MEN

While narcissistic abuse can affect anyone, men often face unique challenges that can make recognizing and addressing the abuse more difficult.

- **Societal Expectations**: Societal norms and expectations may discourage men from expressing vulnerability or seeking help.

- **Stigma**: Men may fear judgment or stigma for admitting they are victims of abuse.

- **Isolation**: Men may feel isolated or believe they are alone in their experiences.

- **Internalized Emotions**: Men may struggle with internalizing their emotions, leading to feelings of shame or inadequacy.

By grasping the essence of narcissistic abuse, its distinct characteristics, and its devastating impact, you empower yourself to identify these patterns in your life. This understanding marks the pivotal first step towards breaking free from the cycle of abuse and embarking on a healing journey. Knowledge equips you with the strength to recognize, resist, and overcome the harmful effects of narcissistic abuse, setting the stage for a brighter, healthier future.

2

Recognizing the Signs

Recognizing the signs of narcissistic behavior can be challenging, especially when the narcissist's actions are subtle or covert. Here are some common red flags and warning signs to watch out for:

1. Red Flags and Warning Signs

- Blaming the victim for things they didn't do, making them feel guilty or responsible.
- Separating the victim from friends and family to increase dependence on the manipulator.
- Restricting access to finances or resources to make the victim dependent on the abuser.
- Narcissists crave constant validation and admiration from others. They thrive on

attention and become agitated or angry when they don't receive it.

- They often exploit others for personal gain, whether emotionally, financially, or socially.
- They believe they are superior to others and deserve special treatment and expect others to cater to their needs without question.
- They often dominate conversations, seeking to be the center of attention. If they feel ignored or undervalued, they may become upset or angry.
- They might tell different things to different people to cause conflict or competition between them.
- Narcissists may bring another person into the relationship to make the original person feel jealous or insecure. By keeping people divided and unsure of each other, the narcissists maintain control over the situation and the people involved, and can gain support and validation for their perspective.
- They try to dictate how others should think, feel, or act, often ignoring others' autonomy.
- They may say or do things without considering the impact on others, leading to unintentional harm.
- They find it difficult to forgive others, even when apologies are made or amends are

attempted. They often remember old conflicts. Sometimes Seek revenge.

+ They often create tension in relationships due to unrealistic expectations and criticism.

+ Narcissists may struggle to understand or care about the feelings and needs of others. They might be insensitive to others' emotions and perspectives.

+ Even minor criticism can provoke strong reactions. Viewing it as a personal attack, they might become defensive or aggressive.

+ They may overstate their accomplishments and abilities to impress others and reinforce their sense of superiority.

+ They rarely take responsibility for their actions and often blame others for their problems.

+ They can be charming and engaging (overwhelming the victim with affection, gifts, and attention), but this charm is often used to create dependency.

+ They use lies to manipulate others and control situations to their advantage without feeling guilty or remorseful about deceiving others.

+ They may become extremely jealous and possessive in relationships.

+ They may become easily frustrated and impatient, especially when things don't go their way.

- Constantly feel unsatisfied and crave more, no matter what they achieve or receive.
- Their decisions are often based on what benefits them, with little regard for others.
- They may not feel guilt or remorse for their actions, even if they hurt others.
- They rarely take responsibility for their mistakes and may deflect blame onto others.
- They may thrive on chaos and conflict, often creating drama in their relationships.
- They may only hear what they want to hear, ignoring important details or feedback.
- They can put others down to boost their own ego.
- They can develop addictions to substances, work, or other activities as a way to cope with their insecurities.
- They may struggle to admit when they are wrong or offer sincere apologies.
- They see themselves as perpetual victims, blaming others for their problems.
- They may have trouble accepting truths that do not align with their grandiose self-image.
- They may dismiss others' opinions, feelings, or contributions as unimportant.
- They may have trouble trusting others and may constantly doubt others' intentions.

- ♦ They make the victim doubt their own reality, memories, or perceptions
- ♦ They often use silent treatment (withdrawing communication and affection) as a form of punishment or control.
- ♦ Emotional Instability: Narcissists actions and attitudes can change rapidly and unexpectedly. Alternating charm and hostility. Their unpredictable moods can create tension and confusion in relationships, as others may feel like they are "walking on eggshells."

2. Emotional and Psychological Impact

The effects of narcissistic abuse can be deeply damaging to a victim's emotional and psychological well-being. Understanding these impacts can help victims recognize the abuse and seek help:

- **Emotional Trauma**: Victims often experience intense feelings of fear, anxiety, depression, and hopelessness. The constant manipulation and emotional abuse can lead to complex post-traumatic stress disorder (C-PTSD).

- **Self-Doubt and Confusion**: Narcissistic abuse erodes a victim's sense of reality and self-worth, leading to pervasive self-doubt and confusion. Victims may question their own perceptions and judgments, making it difficult to trust themselves.

- **Isolation**: Narcissists often isolate their victims from friends, family, and support networks, leaving them feeling alone and unsupported. This isolation makes it harder for victims to seek help and escape the abusive situation.

- **Physical Health Issues**: The chronic stress and emotional turmoil caused by narcissistic abuse can lead to physical health problems, such as headaches, insomnia, digestive issues, and weakened immune function.

- **Anxiety**: Constant fear and worry about the abuser's reactions, leading to heightened levels of anxiety and panic attacks.

- **Hypervigilance**: Being overly alert and sensitive to potential threats, leading to constant stress and exhaustion.

- **Trust Issues**: Difficulty trusting others and forming healthy relationships due to the betrayal and manipulation experienced during the abuse.

- **Difficulty Establishing Boundaries**: Struggling to set and maintain healthy boundaries in future relationships, often resulting in further manipulation and abuse.

3. Personal Stories and Case Studies

Personal stories and case studies provide valuable insights into the dynamics of narcissistic abuse and its impact on victims. These narratives illustrate the various ways narcissistic behavior manifests and the profound effects it has on those involved:

1. John's Journey to_Freedom

- I was in a relationship with someone who constantly belittled and controlled me. My partner criticized everything I did, mocked my interests, and downplayed my achievements. This made me feel worthless and inadequate over time.

- She also isolated me from my friends and family, dictating who I could see and when. They created conflicts to keep me away from my support network and monitored my activities, questioning my every move. I felt like I had no privacy or autonomy.

- At first, I didn't see the red flags. I thought my partner was just having bad days. But as the manipulation got worse, I began to see a pattern. I researched narcissistic behavior and sought support from friends and professionals.

- With this new understanding, I started setting boundaries and standing up for myself. It was tough, but I knew I had to break free. Eventually, I made the hard decision to leave the relationship. Now, I'm focused on healing, rebuilding my life, and helping others recognize and escape toxic relationships.

- My experience taught me the importance of self-worth and the courage it takes to reclaim your life. If you're in a similar situation, know that you deserve better and can find the strength to break free.

2. Michael's Journey to Freedom

- I worked under a boss who constantly manipulated me in various ways. They often took credit for my successes, downplaying my contributions and making it seem like their ideas. This left me feeling unappreciated and undervalued.

- The boss also micromanaged my tasks, giving me unnecessary, detailed instructions that undermined my skills and autonomy. It was as if they didn't trust me to handle even the simplest of tasks.

- Additionally, they spread negative rumors about me to colleagues, damaging my reputation and creating a hostile work environment. This isolation made it difficult to build supportive relationships at work.

- At first, I didn't see these behaviors as red flags. I thought my boss was just demanding. But as the manipulation became clearer, I realized I was in a toxic situation. I researched narcissistic behavior and sought advice from friends and mentors.

- With this understanding, I started setting boundaries and standing up for myself. It wasn't easy, but I knew I had to protect my well-being. Eventually, I made the tough decision to leave the job.

- Now, I am using this experience to seek out healthier work environments. It's a journey of rebuilding confidence and finding balance. By sharing my story, I hope to help others see the signs of a toxic workplace and emphasize the importance of mental health and self-respect.

- My experience showed me how important it is to have the courage to make a change and the importance of putting my mental and emotional health first.

3. Joe's Journey to Self-Worth

- Growing up with a narcissistic parent, Joe faced constant emotional manipulation. His parent's relentless need for control and validation left him feeling insignificant and unworthy. Joe's achievements were either dismissed or taken credit for, and his feelings were often invalidated.

- The psychological impact was profound. Joe struggled with low self-esteem, anxiety, and a lack of identity. He often questioned his self-worth and found it difficult to trust others.

- Joe's path to healing began with acknowledging the toxicity of his upbringing. He sought therapy, where he learned to identify and challenge the negative beliefs instilled in him. Through this process, Joe began to rebuild his self-esteem and establish healthy boundaries.

- Connecting with supportive friends and mentors was crucial. They offered validation and encouragement, helping Joe see his true value. Engaging in activities that brought him joy and fulfillment also played a significant role in his recovery.

- Over time, Joe's sense of self-worth grew stronger. He learned to prioritize his well-being and make decisions that aligned with his values. Sharing his story became a way to help others understand the impact of narcissistic parenting and the importance of self-worth.

- Joe's journey is a powerful reminder that healing and growth are possible, even after a difficult upbringing. It's a testament to the resilience of the human spirit and the transformative power of self-acceptance.

4. Unique Experiences of Men

Men may experience narcissistic abuse differently due to societal expectations and stereotypes. Here are some unique experiences men might face:

- **Minimization of Abuse**: Men may feel that their experiences are minimized or not taken seriously because of societal norms that expect men to be strong and self-reliant.

- **Fear of Judgment**: Men may fear being judged or perceived as weak for admitting they are victims of abuse.

- **Internalized Emotions**: Men may struggle with expressing their emotions, leading to internalized feelings of shame, guilt, and confusion.

- **Difficulty Seeking Help**: Men may find it challenging to seek help due to the stigma associated with being a male victim of abuse.

By recognizing the signs and understanding the impact of narcissistic abuse, you will be better equipped to identify and address these behaviors in your own lives. This knowledge empowers you to take the necessary steps toward healing and recovery.

3

Breaking Free

Breaking free from a narcissistic relationship is a challenging and courageous step. It requires careful planning, support, and a strong resolve. This chapter provides practical advice and strategies to help you safely and effectively end the relationship and begin your journey towards healing.

Acknowledging the Need to Leave

The first and often most difficult step is acknowledging the need to leave the relationship. Narcissists are skilled at creating a false sense of security and dependence, making it hard to see the toxic nature of the relationship. Recognizing the detrimental impact on your mental and emotional well-being is crucial. Trust your instincts and understand that you deserve a life free from manipulation and abuse.

1. Identifying and writing down the signs

Recognizing the signs of narcissistic abuse is the first step towards addressing and overcoming it. Here are some strategies to help you identify and respond to the abuse:

- **Keep a Journal**: Document incidents of abusive behavior, noting the date, time, and details. This can help you see patterns and validate your experiences.

- **Seek Validation**: Talk to trusted friends, family members, or support groups about your experiences. Their validation can help you recognize the abuse.

- **Educate Yourself**: Learn about narcissistic abuse and its effects through books, articles, and reputable websites.

- **Trust Your Instincts**: If something feels wrong, trust your instincts. Your feelings and experiences are valid.

- **Set Boundaries**: Establish and maintain clear boundaries with the abuser to protect yourself.

- **Seek Professional Help**: Consider seeking therapy or counseling to help you process your experiences and develop coping strategies.

Men may face unique challenges in identifying and addressing abuse due to societal expectations and stigma.

Strategies such as journaling, seeking validation, and educating yourself can help you recognize and respond to the abuse.

2. <u>Preparing to Leave</u>

Preparation is key to safely and successfully leaving a narcissistic relationship. Here are some important steps to take

- **Build a Support System**: Reach out to trusted friends, family members, or support groups. Having a network of people who understand your situation and can provide emotional and practical support is essential.

- **Gather Evidence**: Document instances of abuse, manipulation, and control. This evidence can be useful if you need to take legal action or seek protection.

- **Plan Your Exit**: Create a detailed plan for leaving, including where you will go, how you will get there, and what you need to take with you. Have a safe place to stay, such as a friend's house, a family member's home, or a shelter.

- **Financial Independence**: Secure your finances by opening a separate bank account, saving money, and ensuring you have access to essential documents like identification, insurance papers, and financial records.

3. Legal and Safety Considerations

Leaving a narcissistic relationship may involve legal and safety concerns, especially if the narcissist is likely to retaliate. Consider the following:

- **Restraining Orders**: If you fear for your safety, seek a restraining order or protective order to keep the narcissist away from you.

- **Legal Advice**: Consult with a lawyer to understand your rights and the legal steps you can take to protect yourself, especially if there are shared assets, children, or other legal matters involved.

- **Safety Plan**: Develop a safety plan that includes emergency contacts, safe locations, and steps to take if you are in immediate danger. Keep this plan accessible and share it with trusted individuals.

4. **Emotional Preparation**

Leaving a narcissistic relationship is not only a physical separation but also an emotional journey. Prepare yourself emotionally by:

- **Setting Boundaries**: Establish clear boundaries with the narcissist. Limit or cut off communication to prevent further manipulation and control.

- **Therapy and Counseling**: Seek professional help from a therapist or counselor who specializes in narcissistic abuse. Therapy can provide you with coping strategies, emotional support, and guidance through the healing process.

- **Self-Care**: Prioritize self-care and self-compassion. Engage in activities that bring you joy, relaxation, and a sense of well-being. Rebuild your self-esteem and confidence through positive affirmations and self-reflection.

Once you have successfully left the narcissistic relationship, focus on rebuilding your life and healing from the trauma.

4

Healing and Recovery

Healing from narcissistic abuse is a multi-faceted and deeply personal journey. This chapter provides strategies and insights to help you navigate the path to recovery and rebuild your sense of self-worth and well-being.

Acknowledging the Pain

The first step in the healing process is acknowledging the pain and trauma you have experienced. Narcissistic abuse can leave deep emotional scars, and it's important to validate your feelings and recognize that your pain is real and justified. Allow yourself to grieve the loss of the relationship and the impact it has had on your life.

1. a) Self-Care and Self-Compassion

Self-care and self-compassion are essential components of healing. They help you reconnect with yourself and nurture your emotional and physical well-being. Here are some self-care practices to consider:

- **Mindfulness and Meditation**: Practicing mindfulness and meditation can help you stay grounded and present.

These practices can reduce stress, anxiety, and negative thought patterns, allowing you to focus on your healing journey.

- **Physical Self-Care**: Taking care of your physical health is crucial. Engage in regular exercise, maintain a balanced diet, and ensure you get enough sleep. These activities can boost your mood and energy levels.

- **Emotional Self-Care**: Engage in activities that bring you joy and relaxation. This can include hobbies, creative pursuits, or spending time in nature. Allow yourself to experience positive emotions and find comfort in the things you love.

- **Boundaries**: Establish and maintain healthy boundaries with others. This includes limiting contact with the narcissist and protecting your emotional space. Boundaries are essential for safeguarding your well-being and preventing further harm.

1. b) Seeking Professional Help

Therapy and counseling can play a vital role in your recovery. A therapist who specializes in narcissistic abuse can provide you with the tools and support you need to heal. Consider the following therapeutic approaches:

- **Cognitive Behavioral Therapy (CBT)**: CBT can help you identify and change negative thought patterns and behaviors. It is effective in addressing anxiety, depression, and trauma related to narcissistic abuse.

- **Eye Movement Desensitization and Reprocessing (EMDR)**: EMDR is a specialized therapy for trauma. It can help you process and heal from the traumatic experiences of narcissistic abuse.

- **Group Therapy**: Joining a support group with other survivors of narcissistic abuse can provide a sense of community and shared understanding. Group therapy offers validation, support, and encouragement from others who have experienced similar situations.

2. Rebuilding Self-Esteem and Confidence

Narcissistic abuse often leaves victims with low self-esteem and a diminished sense of self-worth. Rebuilding your self-esteem is a crucial part of the healing process. Here are some strategies to help you regain confidence:

- **Positive Affirmations**: Use positive affirmations to challenge negative self-beliefs and reinforce your worth. Repeat statements like, "I am worthy of love and respect," and "I am strong and capable."

- **Self-Reflection**: Reflect on your strengths, achievements, and qualities. Write them down and remind yourself of your value. Celebrate your progress and acknowledge your resilience.

- **Personal Goals**: Set small, achievable goals that align with your interests and passions. Accomplishing these goals can boost your confidence and provide a sense of purpose and fulfillment.

- **Surround Yourself with Positivity**: Surround yourself with supportive and positive people who uplift and encourage you. Avoid individuals who may undermine your self-worth or bring negativity into your life.

3. Reconnecting with Your Self-essence

Narcissistic abuse can cause you to lose touch with your true self. Reconnecting with your authentic self involves rediscovering your passions, values, and identity. Here are some steps to help you on this journey:

- **Journaling**: Keep a journal to explore your thoughts, feelings, and experiences. Journaling can provide clarity and insight into your inner world, helping you reconnect with your true self.

- **Creative Expression**: Engage in creative activities that allow you to express yourself, such as painting, writing, music, or dance. Creative expression can be a powerful tool for healing and self-discovery.

- **Rediscovering Passions**: Revisit hobbies and interests that you may have neglected during the relationship. Pursuing activities that bring you joy and fulfillment can help you reconnect with your passions.

4. Building a Support Network

A strong support network is essential for your healing journey. Surround yourself with people who understand and validate your experiences. Here are some ways to build a supportive community:

- **Friends and Family**: Reach out to trusted friends and family members who can provide emotional support and encouragement. Share your experiences and lean on them for comfort and understanding.

- **Support Groups**: Join support groups or online communities for survivors of narcissistic abuse. These groups offer a safe space to share your story, gain insights, and connect with others who have faced similar challenges.

- **Professional Support**: In addition to therapy, consider seeking support from coaches, mentors, or spiritual advisors who can guide you on your healing journey.

Breaking Down Barriers to Men's Assistance

The societal expectations and stigmas that surround masculinity create distinct challenges for men who seek support, often making them feel that they must handle their issues alone. These pressures can be overwhelming, discouraging men from pursuing the assistance they deserve for their mental and emotional well-being. Here are some strategies to overcome them:

Addressing Stigma: Challenge societal norms that discourage men from seeking help. Remember, seeking support is a sign of strength, not weakness. Educate yourself and others about the benefits of seeking help, and openly discuss mental health to normalize the conversation.

Breaking Down Barriers: Recognize and address internal barriers, such as fear of judgment or feelings of shame. Understand that your experiences are valid, and you deserve support. Practice self-compassion and remind yourself that seeking help is a courageous act.

Encouraging Self-Advocacy: Empower yourself to advocate for your needs. Seek out resources and support that align with your values and preferences. Research available options, whether it's therapy, support groups, or online communities, and find what works best for you. Take an active role in your healing journey by voicing your needs and setting personal goals

Educating Yourself and Others: Knowledge is power. Learning about narcissistic abuse and sharing what you've learned with others can help raise awareness and reduce stigma. Education fosters understanding and creates a more supportive environment for everyone.

Overcoming barriers to seeking support is essential for your mental and emotional well-being. By challenging societal stigma, breaking down internal barriers, and advocating for personal needs, you can find the courage to seek help.

Building a support network, practicing self-care, and seeking professional guidance are key strategies. Setting boundaries protects your emotional well-being by defining what is acceptable in interactions. Celebrating small achievements boosts your confidence and reinforces positive behavior.

Educating oneself and others about narcissistic abuse fosters a supportive environment for all. As a community, we can stand together, offering encouragement and strength. You are not alone—there is a network of survivors and allies ready to support you every step of the way.

Moving Forward with Resilience

Healing from narcissistic abuse is a gradual and ongoing process. Embrace the journey with patience and self-compassion. Celebrate your progress, no matter how small, and recognize the strength and resilience you possess. Here are some final thoughts to guide you forward:

- **Embrace Change**: Accept that change is a natural part of the healing process. Allow yourself to grow and evolve as you move forward.

- **Focus on the Present**: While it's important to acknowledge the past, focus on the present and the future. Create a vision for the life you want to build and take steps towards it each day.

- **Practice Self-Love**: Cultivate a deep sense of self-love and acceptance. Treat yourself with kindness and compassion, and prioritize your well-being.

- **Seek Joy**: Seek joy and fulfillment in everyday moments. Engage in activities that bring you happiness and surround yourself with positivity.

Your journey of healing and recovery is a testament to your courage and resilience. By taking these steps, you are reclaiming your life and paving the way for a brighter, healthier, and more fulfilling future.

5

Rebuilding Your Life

Rebuilding your life after experiencing narcissistic abuse is a powerful and transformative journey. It involves rediscovering your true self, establishing healthy boundaries, and creating a fulfilling and joyful future. This chapter provides guidance and strategies to help you rebuild your life and thrive.

1. Establishing Healthy Boundaries

Healthy boundaries are essential for protecting your well-being and preventing future abuse. They help you define what is acceptable and unacceptable behavior from others. Here are some steps to establish and maintain healthy boundaries:

- **Identify Your Limits**: Reflect on your physical, emotional, and mental limits. What behaviors make you feel uncomfortable or disrespected? Knowing your limits is the first step to setting boundaries.

- **Communicate Clearly**: Assertively communicate your boundaries to others. Use "I" statements to express your needs and feelings, such as "I feel uncomfortable when you raise your voice. Please speak to me calmly."

- **Be Consistent**: Consistency is key to maintaining boundaries. Enforce your boundaries every time they are crossed, and do not make exceptions for certain people or situations.

- **Practice Self-Respect**: Respect your own boundaries and prioritize your well-being. Do not feel guilty for saying no or protecting your space.

2. Reconnecting with Yourself

Narcissistic abuse can cause you to lose touch with your true self. Reconnecting with who you are involves exploring your passions, values, and identity. Here are some ways to reconnect with yourself:

- **Self-Reflection**: Take time to reflect on your experiences, values, and goals. Journaling can be a helpful tool for self-reflection and gaining clarity about what is important to you.

- **Pursue Your Interests**: Revisit hobbies and activities that bring you joy and fulfillment. Engaging in activities you love can help you reconnect with your passions and rediscover your sense of self.

- **Set Personal Goals**: Identify personal goals that align with your values and interests. Working towards these goals can provide a sense of purpose and direction in your life.

- **Embrace Your Authentic Self**: Celebrate your uniqueness and embrace your authentic self. Let go of any pressure to conform to others' expectations and be true to who you are.

3. Building a Support System

A strong support system is crucial for your healing and growth. Surround yourself with people who uplift and encourage you. Here are some ways to build and nurture your support network:

- **Reconnect with Loved Ones**: specially those who understand and support you

- **Join Support Groups**: learn from others victims' victory may help you a lot

- **Seek Professional Help**: for accompanying you and your journey

- **Establish New Connections**: Meet new people who share your interests and values. Building new relationships can expand your support network and provide fresh perspectives.

4. Pursuing Personal Growth

Personal growth is a continuous and rewarding journey. Embrace opportunities for learning, self-improvement, and development. Here are some ways to pursue personal growth:

- **Education and Skill Development**: Consider taking courses or workshops to learn new skills or further your education. Continuous learning can boost your confidence and open up new opportunities.

- **Mindfulness and Self-Awareness**: Practice mindfulness to stay present and aware of your thoughts, feelings, and actions. Mindfulness can help you develop a deeper understanding of yourself and your experiences.

- **Emotional Intelligence**: Work on developing your emotional intelligence by recognizing and managing your emotions, as well as understanding and empathizing with others' feelings.

- **Self-Compassion**: Practice self-compassion by treating yourself with kindness and understanding. Acknowledge your strengths and accomplishments, and forgive yourself for any perceived mistakes.

5. Creating a Fulfilling Future

As you rebuild your life, focus on creating a future that brings you happiness and fulfillment. Here are some steps to help you achieve this:

- **Set Clear Goals**: Define your short-term and long-term goals. Break them down into manageable steps and celebrate your progress along the way.

- **Cultivate Positive Habits**: Develop positive habits that support your well-being and personal growth. This can include regular exercise, healthy eating, and mindfulness practices.

- **Surround Yourself with Positivity**: Create a positive environment by surrounding yourself with people, activities, and experiences that uplift and inspire you.

- **Embrace Change**: Be open to change and new opportunities. Embracing change can lead to personal growth and new experiences that enrich your life.

- **Celebrate Your Journey**: Acknowledge and celebrate your journey of healing and rebuilding. Recognize your achievements and the progress you have made, no matter how small.

Moving Forward with Resilience

Rebuilding your life after narcissistic abuse is a testament to your strength and resilience. Embrace the journey with patience and self-compassion. Remember that recovery is a gradual process, and it's okay to seek help and support along the way.

By taking these steps, you are creating a brighter, healthier, and more fulfilling future for yourself. Celebrate your progress, honor your journey, and continue to move forward with courage and determination.

6

Moving Forward

Moving forward after experiencing narcissistic abuse is a journey of growth, healing, and rediscovery. This chapter provides guidance on how to embrace a brighter future, avoid falling into old patterns, and cultivate a life filled with joy and fulfillment.

A- Be kind and patient with yourself

Being kind and patient with yourself allows you to face challenges with grace and resilience. It nurtures a positive mindset, making room for healing and personal growth.

a) **Embracing Change:** Change can be both daunting and liberating. Embrace the changes that come with moving forward by adopting a positive and open mindset.

b) **Accept the Past**: Acknowledge your past experiences without letting them define you. Understand that the past is a part of your story, but it does not have to dictate your future.

c) **Adopt a Growth Mindset**: Embrace challenges as opportunities for growth. View setbacks as learning experiences and believe in your ability to overcome obstacles.

d) **Be Open to New Experiences**: Allow yourself to explore new interests, meet new people, and try new activities. New experiences can lead to personal growth and fulfillment.

B. Cultivating Self-Compassion

Self-compassion is vital for moving forward with resilience and strength. Treat yourself with kindness and understanding as you navigate your healing journey:

- **Practice Self-Forgiveness**: Let go of any guilt or self-blame related to the abuse. Forgive yourself for any perceived mistakes and understand that you did the best you could in a difficult situation.

- **Celebrate Small Wins**: Recognize and celebrate your progress, no matter how small. Every step forward is an achievement worth acknowledging.

- **Be Gentle with Yourself**: Healing takes time, and it's okay to have ups and downs. Be patient and gentle with yourself as you navigate this journey.

◆ Building Healthy Relationships

Healthy relationships are built on mutual respect, trust, and understanding. Moving forward involves fostering positive connections and avoiding toxic dynamics:

- **Set Clear Boundaries**: Establish and maintain healthy boundaries in all your relationships. Communicate your needs and limits clearly and assertively.

- **Choose Supportive People**: Surround yourself with individuals who respect and support you. Avoid those who exhibit narcissistic traits or engage in manipulative behaviors.

- **Build Trust Gradually**: Trust is built over time. Allow relationships to develop naturally and avoid rushing into new connections.

Recognizing and embracing personal growth.

A- Pursuing Personal Passions

Rediscovering and pursuing your passions can bring joy and fulfillment to your life. Focus on activities that resonate with your interests and values:

- **Identify Your Interests**: Reflect on what brings you joy and fulfillment. Make a list of hobbies, activities, and pursuits that excite you.

- **Set Personal Goals**: Define clear and achievable goals related to your interests. Break them down into manageable steps and celebrate your progress.

- **Make Time for Enjoyment**: Prioritize activities that bring you happiness. Schedule regular time for hobbies and interests that nurture your soul.

B- Prioritizing Self-Care

Self-care is essential for maintaining your well-being and preventing burnout. Incorporate self-care practices into your daily routine:

- **Physical Self-Care**: Engage in regular exercise, maintain a balanced diet, and ensure you get enough rest. Physical well-being supports emotional and mental health.

- **Emotional Self-Care**: Allow yourself to feel and process your emotions. Seek support from friends, family, or a therapist when needed.

- **Mental Self-Care**: Practice mindfulness, meditation, and stress-reduction techniques. Keep your mind engaged with activities that stimulate and challenge you.

C- Finding Purpose and Meaning

Moving forward involves finding purpose and meaning in your life. Identify what gives you a sense of fulfillment and direction:

- **Reflect on Your Values**: Consider what values are important to you. Align your actions and decisions with these values.

- **Contribute to Others**: Engage in activities that allow you to give back to others. Volunteering, mentoring, or helping those in need can bring a sense of purpose.

- **Create a Vision for Your Future**: Envision the life you want to build. Set long-term goals and create a plan to achieve them. Stay focused on your vision and take steps towards it each day.

Embracing Resilience

Resilience is the ability to bounce back from adversity and continue moving forward. Cultivate resilience by embracing your inner strength:

- **Develop Coping Strategies**: Identify healthy coping mechanisms that help you manage stress and challenges.

This can include journaling, talking to a friend, or engaging in a relaxing activity.

- **Stay Connected**: Maintain strong connections with supportive individuals. Lean on your support network during difficult times.

- **Focus on the Positive**: Shift your focus towards positive aspects of your life. Practice gratitude and acknowledge the good things, no matter how small.

◆ Exercises Specifically for Men

Men may benefit from tailored exercises that address their unique experiences and challenges. Here are some exercises to consider:

- **Journaling**: Keeping a journal can help you process your thoughts and emotions. Write about your experiences, reflect on your progress, and set goals for the future.

- **Affirmations**: Practice positive affirmations to boost your self-esteem and counteract negative self-talk. Repeat affirmations such as:

a. "I am worthy of love and respect"

b. "I have the strength to overcome challenges"

c. I am capable and confident."

d. "I am healing and growing every day."

e. "I deserve happiness and fulfillment."

- **Visualization**: Use visualization techniques to imagine a future where you have healed from the abuse. Picture yourself feeling confident, happy, and free from the effects of the abuse.

- **Breathing Exercises**: Practice deep breathing exercises to calm your mind and reduce stress. Techniques such as diaphragmatic breathing or the 4-7-8 method can be particularly effective.

Moving forward after narcissistic abuse is a journey of transformation and empowerment. Embrace each step with courage and determination. As you rebuild your life, remember that you have the strength to create a future filled with joy, fulfillment, and meaningful connections.

Celebrate your progress, honor your resilience, and continue to move forward with hope and optimism. Your journey is a testament to your inner strength and the incredible possibilities that lie ahead.

CONCLUSION

As we reach the end of **" Narcissistic Abuse Recovery,"** it's important to reflect on the journey you've embarked upon. Healing from narcissistic abuse is a profound and courageous process, one that requires strength, resilience, and unwavering determination. By reading this book, you have taken a significant step toward reclaiming your life and embracing a brighter future.

Reflecting on Your Journey

The journey of healing from narcissistic abuse is not linear. It is filled with ups and downs, moments of clarity, and times of uncertainty. Throughout this book, you have gained a deeper understanding of narcissistic abuse, learned to recognize the signs, and explored practical strategies for breaking free and rebuilding your life.

Remember that healing is a gradual process. It's okay to take small steps and celebrate every victory, no matter how minor it may seem. Acknowledge your progress and be gentle with yourself as you continue to navigate this journey.

Embracing Your Strength

Surviving and recovering from narcissistic abuse is a testament to your inner strength and resilience. You have faced tremendous challenges and have emerged stronger and wiser. Embrace your strength and recognize the incredible courage it takes to confront and heal from such trauma.

You are not defined by the abuse you have experienced. Instead, you are defined by your ability to rise above it and create a life filled with joy, purpose, and fulfillment. Hold onto the knowledge that you have the power to shape your future and build the life you deserve.

Moving Forward with Hope

As you move forward, carry with you the lessons and insights you have gained. Let them guide you in making healthy choices, setting boundaries, and fostering positive relationships. Trust in your ability to create a life that aligns with your values and aspirations.

Surround yourself with uplifting and motivating people. Seek out resources that aid in your healing and growth. Remember, you are not alone—many others share your journey and offer their support. I'm here with you too, as a fellow survivor of narcissistic abuse.

Together, we can find strength and resilience.

Appendix

A: Worksheets for Self-Reflection and Healing

Self-Reflection Worksheets

1. Identifying Narcissistic Behaviors Worksheet

- **Purpose**: To help recognize and document specific narcissistic behaviors experienced.

- **Instructions**: Reflect on your experiences and answer the following prompts

Question	Response
Describe a situation where you felt manipulated or controlled.	
How did the narcissist make you doubt your own reality or feelings?	
List any behaviors that felt dismissive or demeaning.	
How did these behaviors affect your emotional and mental well-being?	

2. Recognizing Red Flags Worksheet

- **Purpose**: To help identify warning signs of narcissistic behavior.

- **Instructions**: Reflect on your relationships and answer the following prompts.

Question	Response
List the behaviors that initially seemed charming or too good to be true.	
Identify any instances where you felt excessively criticized or belittled.	
How did the narcissist react when you tried to set boundaries?	
Describe moments when you felt isolated from friends or family.	

3. Emotional Impact Assessment Worksheet

- **Purpose**: To assess the emotional and psychological impact of the abuse.

- **Instructions**: Reflect on your feelings and answer the following prompts. Use a scale of 1-10 (1 = not at all, 10 = extremely) where applicable.

Question	Response
How often do you feel anxious or fearful? (1-10)	
How often do you feel depressed or hopeless? (1-10)	
How much do you doubt your own perceptions and judgments? (1-10)	
Describe the physical symptoms you have experienced (e.g., headaches, insomnia).	

B: Journaling Prompts

1. Healing and Growth Prompts

Prompt	Response
How did the abuse make you feel?	
What emotions are you experiencing today?	
What small victories have you accomplished this week?	
How have you grown since leaving the abusive relationship?	
What does a fulfilling life look like to you?	
What steps can you take to achieve your vision?	

2. Self-Discovery Prompts

Prompt	Response
What activities bring you joy?	
What hobbies did you enjoy before the abusive relationship?	
What values are most important to you?	
How can you align your actions with your values?	
What are your greatest strengths?	
How have your strengths helped you navigate your journey?	

C: Affirmations and Positive Quotes

1. Affirmations for Healing and Recovery

I can overcome any challenge.
I am worthy of love and respect.
I deserve happiness and fulfillment.
I trust my instincts and believe in myself.
I believe in my ability to restore and excel.
I am healing and growing stronger every day.
I have the power to create a safe and joyful life.
I am not defined by someone else's opinion of me.
I forgive my past mistakes and stride forward steadily.
I attract positive and healthy relationships into my life.
I believe in my capacity to overcome, heal and succeed.

2. Positive Quotes

Quote	Reflect On
"The only way out is through."	[ ]
"You are stronger than you know."	[ ]
"Healing takes time, and asking for help is a courageous step."	[ ]
"Every small step counts in your journey to recovery	[ ]
"Your story is not over yet."	[ ]
"Believe in yourself and all that you are."	[ ]

Appendix E: Frequently Asked Questions (FAQs)

1) Common Questions About Narcissistic Abuse

Question	Answer
What are the signs of narcissistic behavior?	Some of them: an excessive need for attention and admiration, lack of empathy, manipulative behavior, grandiosity, emotional instability, paranoia, self-victimization.
How can I safely leave a narcissistic relationship?	Prepare by building a support system, gathering evidence, planning your exit, securing financial independence, and seeking legal advice if necessary.
What are the long-term effects of narcissistic abuse?	Long-term effects can include emotional trauma, low self-esteem, anxiety, depression, isolation, and physical health issues.

2) Questions About Healing and Recovery

Question	Answer
How can I rebuild my self-esteem after abuse?	Use positive affirmations, reflect on your strengths and achievements, set personal goals, and surround yourself with supportive people.
What are effective strategies for coping with trauma?	Strategies include seeking therapy, practicing mindfulness and meditation, engaging in self-care activities, and joining support groups.
How can I recognize and avoid future narcissistic relationships?	Learn to identify red flags and warning signs, establish and maintain healthy boundaries, and trust your instincts.

NOTES